CAThletics

Books by Jo and Paul Loeb

Paul Loeb's Complete Book of Dog Training

The Leather Book

You CAN Train Your Cat

Supertraining Your Dog

CAThletics

CAThletics
Ways to Amuse
and Exercise Your Cat
Jo and Paul Loeb

Line drawings by George Rhoads

Prentice-Hall, Inc., Englewood Cliffs, New Jersey

CAThletics: Ways to Amuse and Exercise Your Cat
by Jo and Paul Loeb
Copyright © 1981 by Jo and Paul Loeb

Address inquiries to Prentice-Hall, Inc.,
Englewood Cliffs, N.J. 07632
Printed in the United States of America
Prentice-Hall International, Inc., London
Prentice-Hall of Australia, Pty. Ltd., Sydney
Prentice-Hall of Canada, Ltd., Toronto
Prentice-Hall of India Private Ltd., New Delhi
Prentice-Hall of Japan, Inc., Tokyo
Prentice-Hall of Southeast Asia Pt. Ltd., Singapore
Whitehall Books Limited, Wellington, New Zealand
10 9 8 7 6 5 4 3 2 1

Library of Congress Cataloging in Publication Data
Loeb, Jo, date
    Cathletics: ways to amuse and exercise your cat.
    1. Cats.   II. Loeb, Paul, date   joint author.
II. Title.
SF447.L62   636.8'0887   80-39813
ISBN 0-13-121004-1

To our daughter, Stephanie, and our pets
Inches, Sleepy, Snap, and Plum

Contents

CAThletics

1. WHY CATHLETICS?

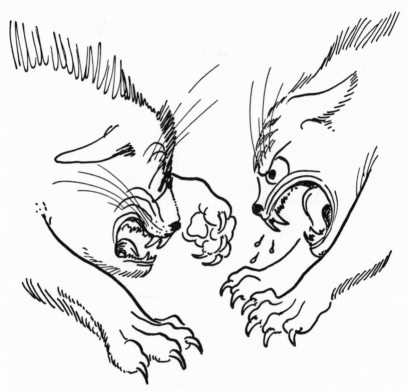

The best exercise for a cat is another cat

One great advantage to cats is that you don't have to walk them outside, the way you must with dogs. Cats, therefore, are the perfect pets for people who have to work all day, or who have apartments. Even in the suburbs, many people keep their cats indoors to protect them from traffic and other animals.

And therein lies the great problem for the indoor cat; lack of stimulation and exercise. All too often, owner and cat lose interest in each other. The cat's appetite suffers, he becomes increasingly finicky, he is more prone to premature aging and illnesses like cancer and heart disease. He sleeps most of the day. If he plays at all, it's by himself. He'll sit in the corner and stare at shadows, trying to catch them with his paws. Your house plants have become targets for his attention because he's got nothing else to do. If he becomes active at all, it's in the middle of the night when you're trying to sleep.

The best exercise for a cat is another cat; a sib-cat keeps a single cat from getting neurotic, going on hunger strikes, and wailing loudly at night. Two or three cats will wrestle, chase each other, sleep together, and console each other when catparents bring alien beings like dogs or kids into the house. They will stay in the house alone quite happily, if they must, for several days. But how to send solo cats into good healthy sweats?

The Computerized Cat Companion

A pet supply company once wanted to come up with the quintessential toy for cats. All the things a cat was reputed to enjoy, all of a cat's physical abilities, personality quirks, strengths, and idiosyncrasies were fed into a computer, which was programmed to assemble the ultimate in cat toys.

The toy turned out to be an electronic cat-shaped device that ran on wheels. Every morning before leaving for work, the owner was supposed to activate the toy. Then at periodic intervals which the owner could predetermine—ranging from a few minutes to several hours—the machine would spit out balls; make various noises; or run across the floor, trailing enticing objects behind it. All this activity was designed to get the cat to play with the machine as it moved from room to room.

Everyone was really excited; this new toy was antici-pated to blow the lid off the market. Everyone knew how much cat owners loved their pets, and a toy scientifically designed as the ideal cat "playmate" had all the markings of

The quintessential toy for cats

huge success. The pet supply company hired an advertising agency to start a marketing campaign. Everything was ready to go. The only thing left to be done was to demonstrate the toy's effectiveness to the heads of the different corporate departments, the advertising company, and the executives involved in the game's marketing and promotion.

The people who had researched and computerized the information came to supervise and explain. Everyone strained to get a better look at this electronic marvel, the prototype for all that were to follow. The team of test cats were brought in—a half-dozen of different varieties, breeds, sexes, and ages, who would be the first felines to enjoy the new device.

The first cat was placed on the floor as all the executives strained to watch. The toy was activated and started ejecting the plastic balls. One hit the cat in the chest and he ran away.

The inventors made notes. Another cat was brought out. The machine made a soft hissing sound and the cat hissed back.

Uncomfortable murmurs swept through the audience. The inventors laughed nervously and mumbled about "minor modifications," "unusual surroundings," and "spooky animals." They put in a third cat. This time, the machine ejected a toy bird on a string and moved off, trailing the object behind. The cat yawned, lay down, and went to sleep.

To "be fair," the inventors suggested that they move the testing to more intimate surroundings. Cats were left alone in their own homes with video cameras set up to film their reactions. But the tapes revealed the same type of reactions seen in the "live" demonstration. The particular tape that sealed the invention's fate with the chairman of the board depicted a cat sleeping while the "companion" ran all over the apartment, bumping into furniture and knocking over knickknacks.

The project was scrapped. Its inventors had made the mistake (as so many people do) of thinking of cats as loners, amusing themselves on their own, independent, disdainful of the company of humans. An indoor cat shouldn't be treated like a stuffed animal.

All the games in this book have been invented and tested by other cat owners, and *proven* effective. They occupy your cat's senses, stretch his muscles, and give him a good workout to tire him out during the day.

Some are pastimes you already know about; others are wholly original: You can expand on them if you want, but the contents of this book should be enough to keep your cat happy and occupied. In fact, many of these pastimes will challenge him to compete with you and make him feel more your equal—if not your superior.

Guidelines for CAThletics

1. There is no reward or praise for playing; the game *itself* is the reward.

2. Be sure to exploit your cat's senses. Catch his eye, excite his hunting instincts, capitalize on his phenomenal sense of hearing. Since a cat's sense of smell is not as extraordinary as a dog's, you can best encourage him to play by stimulating his eyes and ears.

3. Don't force your cat into the games. Make them enticing and enjoyable, and his curiosity will bring him over to you. Once he knows what's happening, he often will initiate the games himself.

4. Touch and handle your cat. Cats understand physical contact when it comes to play.

5. You can't win all the time, but neither can your cat. There has to be a challenge, and a chance to win or lose.

6. There's no single game that all cats love best. You'll

have to discover for yourself exactly what turns your cat on; then work from there. Let him indicate what he likes—and then develop the game the way *he* wants. Take something he enjoys and elaborate on it. But most of all, do things he likes to do over and over again.

7. Don't forget these games are fun, besides being exercise. If they're not, your cat won't play. You don't need to teach, train, or control your cat—the idea is just for you both to have a good time.

2. GAMES NOT TO PLAY

Left to his own devices, your cat may discover various pastimes that aren't terribly compatible with your household valuables or peace of mind. Worse yet, he may *develop* such games out of the ones you've already taught him. So the following two pastimes are ones you may want to discourage—or forestall.

The Toilet Tissue Treadmill

Every cat will do it once—you hope *only* once—in his life. He discovers that when he paws that big white roll, it will revolve and deliver bounteous folds of soft white paper on the floor for him to play with. And so he paws at it again and again, perhaps even seeing how fast he can make the roll rotate, while the pile of toilet tissue on the floor gets deeper and wider.

    The best way to stop this game, if he persists at it, is to reverse the toilet tissue roll when you replace it so that it unrolls *upward*. If your cat gives it a swat with his paw, it will still rotate, but not unroll. And when not rewarded with more than a single loose sheet, any cat will usually stop playing the game—as any behavioral psychologist will be glad to explain to you.

The Gravity Game

Faced with a new object, a cat has precise ways of finding out about it. First he'll sniff it to find out what it smells like. Then he usually gives it a shove with his paw to see how heavy it is, what it's made of. If it rolls, he usually likes the movement and the noise. So he'll give it another push.

Every cat will do it once—you hope only once

The Gravity Game: place a priceless Ming vase on the mantelpiece

If he—and it—are atop a table, bureau or shelf, the object usually doesn't have far to go before it falls to the floor. More movement! More noise! Once your cat has experienced the thrill of watching a falling object bounce off the floor, he's hooked on the Gravity Game.

The owner of Snooker, a cream-colored alley-cat, thought her cat was so cute when she sat on the kitchen counter lobbing bottle caps, pencils, empty spools of thread, and wine corks off on to the floor. It wasn't so funny, though, when Snooker shattered a conch shell, cracked a Chinese ivory carving, and dented an antique watch by flinging them off her owner's dresser. Your cat can't tell what an object's worth, so stop him immediately if he starts to push things off counters and shelves.

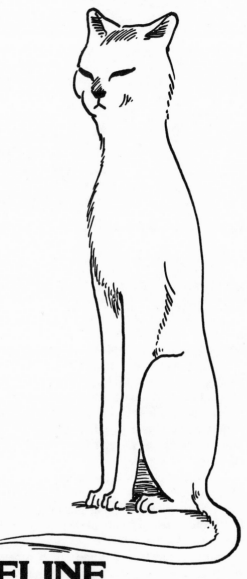

3. FELINE
SOLITAIRE

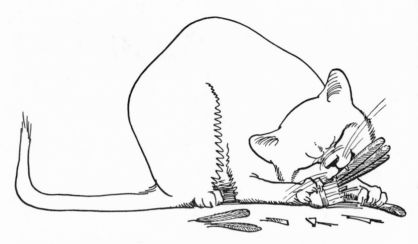

Give your cat objects guaranteed to stay in one piece

If you're going to be away all day at work, be sure to leave your cat some equipment to play with alone, without any interaction on your part. Cats don't much care for rubber balls, toys, imitation mice (unless they are stuffed with catnip), or just about any of the commercially available products. They get more pleasure in "found objects" or things that *you* construct. All they want is for you to remember their instincts and innate characteristics. Keep in mind that cats like things that make noise, move fast, look like interesting prey, are soft enough to chew on, and can be easily moved with the swat of a paw.

The size of a toy is all-important. Cleo, a white female, was given a five-inch red rubber ball when she was just a kitten. She walked over to it, spat at it, and then backed off. Don't forget that *humans* play with objects they can easily manipulate—a basketball or volleyball is about as large as our game projectiles get; and our baseballs, tennis balls, and billiard balls are much smaller. The owner of Undercat, a "former male" with an abundance of extra toes on his front paws, gives him small pieces of newspaper rolled into a ball, which Undercat heartily enjoys. One problem, though: Many cats greatly enjoy ripping paper apart with their teeth. They aren't interested in eating it (you can see them spit it out); they just enjoy the noise and slight resistance the paper offers. So if you don't want to have to clean up a lot of damp confetti, make your ball out of something that will hold together.

Your cat needs something small enough to fit between his paws (when he stretches into the air for an overhead catch) and small enough to carry in his mouth.

On the other hand, you don't want an object so small that he can swallow it. More than one owner has come into a room just in time to find the end of a long piece of string disappearing down the cat's mouth. Similarly, cats find rubber bands irresistible as chewing gum and will often swallow them down—only to vomit them up again later. Don't risk an intestinal blockage; give your cat objects that are too big to swallow and are guaranteed to stay in one piece.

Rug Pucks

Cats of all stripes (and breeds) like to have a small object that they can bat with their paws. The "puck" will go skittering across your floor, and the cat will follow, whacking it up and down the room until he finally loses interest.

If you have hardwood, tile, or linoleum floors, it's best to give your cat something that makes a noise as it rolls. Perhaps the easiest way is to take about a six-inch square of aluminum foil and crumple it into a ball. (Make sure this is unused aluminum foil, right off the roll.) This "silver ball" is small, compact, but also irregular enough to bounce in strange and unexpected ways. Better yet, it's weighty enough to travel some distance after a good shove. Make this the right size so he can easily bat it with his paw and make it scoot across the room.

There are a few drawbacks to aluminum balls. Some cats seem to use them to play a form of miniature golf. Sparky, a small Burmese, has a passion for making holes-in-one. Her owner will find Sparky's silver balls in his litter box, in his water dish—as well as in her shoes in the closet! Another problem is the "taste" of the silver ball. Aluminum isn't exactly flavorful, and many cats get upset when one of their teeth gets stuck in the crumpled foil, as often happens. So you may want to make your cat a softer, chewier ball—one that perhaps won't travel as far, but will be more enjoyable to bite and manipulate.

The Plastic Knotball

Get a plastic bag from the cleaners, or perhaps one of those plastic sheaths in which newsboys wrap their papers on rainy mornings. A plastic bag from the supermarket will also work—but not one that has been used to wrap food. Stretch the plastic into a rope, then tie a knot—and then another. Soon, the accumulation of knots in one place will form an irregular-shaped wad of plastic about an inch thick.

At this point, take a sharp scissors and clip off the remaining plastic on each end. The result will look like one of those small braided rolls you get at the bakery. It will still travel across the rug at good speed, but better still, it responds to the pressure of your cat's jaws and claws. It's far squishier than an aluminum ball; and the more he chews it—leaving little punctures in the plastic—the softer it will become.

Set up a chain-fall of 10,000 dominoes

Tetherball

One unavoidable problem with "pucks" of all sorts is that they quickly disappear, and you'll find yourself making new ones. They'll vanish too. Then one day you'll decide to move out the couch for a good vacuuming, and there, behind it, will be a dozen or more balls that your cat's whacked back there over the past few weeks.

The solution is an ideal solitaire game that was created for Little Cat, a white and yellow fluffball. His owners, who have to work long hours, tied a hollow plastic ball to the closet door knob by a long piece of twine. Little Cat stalks the ball and thwacks it with his paw, whereupon it swings through the air, usually making a satisfying *clack* against the wooden door of the closet. Little Cat's paws keep it in motion, but the string keeps it captive and prevents it from rolling off to where he can't get at it. And its arcs and loops encourage him to leap and stretch—and keep playing longer than if the ball were traveling through a mere two dimensions.

Untethered Balls of Yarn

Cats love to play with balls of wool and don't need anyone to help them. Of course, a ball of string or wool is an age-old feline plaything, overused and hackneyed to the point of being portrayed on greeting cards. Now you can see for yourself the reasons why.

Throw out a ball of twine or wool and your cat will go after it, chasing it all over, rolling on his back, and kicking it into the air. The fact that it's soft and malleable lets him use his claws and teeth without any problem. It is large enough to let him play with it easily, and the fact that it unwinds gives it an organic feeling.

The ball of twine or wool, in fact, "fights back." If it twists around his legs or around the furniture, this entrapment gives your cat the pleasure of having to escape. When he tires of being tangled, he'll leave it alone.

The Stair Game

Since your cat has to provide all the momentum for Rug Pucks, the game seldom lasts more than a few minutes before a cat will tire of it. However, there are ways your cat can use gravity to his advantage.

Mitzi, a beautiful long-haired, white-nosed, black female, lives in a house with a finished basement. Stairs lead up to the kitchen. Mitzi's learned to bring a silver ball to the top step, then drop it, and watch it bounce down the basement stairs. When it's halfway down, she gives chase—and finally corners her metallic prey in a far corner of the basement. Then she brings the ball back upstairs, and the game goes into another round.

Fairly intelligent cats may pick up this stunt on their own, but most cats can be taught it with a bit of persistence on your part.

Stand at the top of the stairs. After your cat comes over to check what's happening, drop a ball and let it bounce down the stairs. When he sees what it is, he'll run down to chase after it. But—whether it's the right size or not—he probably won't bring it back up. If you want to exercise yourself as well as your cat, you can go get the ball for him, run back up the stairs, and roll it down again. Otherwise, take a series of objects with you. This way, you can just sit up there and throw them down until he tires of the game.

4. THE OPENING BUZZERS

Garfield, a grown Manx, goes wild when he hears the sound of crinkling cellophane paper and hunts all over for the source of the sound. (This is probably because cellophane is used so often to wrap food, and he thinks there is some treat in it for him.)

One cat we know has a particular attraction for the sound of a dog barking. Rather than making him run in fear, the sound makes him aggressive. He stands up stiffly and fluffs up his fur. His tail erect, he prowls around on the top of his extended toes, just hankering for a confrontation with the pesky, elusive dog who's invading his territory. (Of course, it is possible that he's putting on a big show for his owner, or just fantasizing—not expecting to see a dog around at all.)

Another cat, Terry, runs from room to room at the sound of a whistle, as if it were the signal to start a race. He'll dash madly around, exhausting himself with a quick burst of energy, and then stops suddenly, lies down, and goes to sleep.

Human races often begin with a pistol shot. Basketball games are punctuated with the blasts on the referee's whistle. Baseball games usually warm up with a recording of the National Anthem. And similarly, you can use noises as signals that it's time to play.

Watch your cat's ears. Even when he's at rest, they'll be moving around, trying to pick up any unusual sounds. Since they move independently, you'll see them going in different directions simultaneously, trying to pinpoint the source of any sounds he might hear.

Even the slightest noise will attract your cat's attention, but certain ones, of course, will entice him more than others. No sudden loud bursts of noise to send him scurrying in fear of his life! What you want to do is to keep your cat on his toes by playing teasing games with sound.

Teach him CATaphonics

Instant Ventriloquism

Wait until he's through resting, then hide somewhere where you can see him. Smack your lips. Blow through your teeth. Kiss the back of your hand. Make a soft Bronx cheer. Scratch or drum on a surface. Make an enticing noise by crinkling paper. Soon he'll lift his ears. His head will pop up and he'll look around to see what's up, his ears swivelling around. Once he pinpoints the sound, he'll either come running with glee, run away, or stealthily stalk over. Wariness is the way a cat will generally react to any strange noises, but sooner or later, his curiosity will bring him around.

Get one of those long cardboard tubes at the center of a roll of gift-wrapping paper. Instant ventriloquism! Any sound you make in one end will be "broadcast" out the other. He'll watch in fascination, trying to figure out what's going on.

Pavlov's Cat

The great Russian psychologist presented a dog with food each time a bell was rung. Soon the ringing of the bell alone had the power to make the dog salivate. (Cats, it should be noted, don't drool that readily. They are more likely to start crying in anticipation, or meowing in a demanding tone. Not as tolerant or patient as dogs, they'll insist on getting what they want.)

See how long it takes your cat to learn to associate a given sound with just about anything you want. To make the association quick and enjoyable, stick with Pavlov's original concept. Start by just ringing a bell or by repeating "food" when you feed your cat. Soon he'll come running to look in his dish when he hears you say the word.

Cats find it easy to grasp—and react to—simple words like "Sit," "Down," and "Good Boy." It's largely a matter of association. Say "Brush," every time you groom your cat, and he'll soon associate the word with the action.

One owner has used this association method to "converse" with his cat, who has learned to associate "food" with canned food, "cookie" with dry food, and "milk" with milk. Thus he can ask the cat which he wants— "food? cookie? milk?"—and gets a meow in reply.

But don't leave it at that; it's too simple. Different words and phrases should signal the start of different games. Ask "What's that?" whenever he investigates something new. Throw a toy and say, "Get the ball." *Any* toy can be a "ball" as far as he's concerned.

5. PURE EXERCISE AND ROUGH-HOUSING

A sudden urge to expend energy

The 100-Room Dash

We once had a little gray cat who loved to run wild. In the middle of the night, when everyone else was sleeping, he'd suddenly leap up and start running. Despite cats' reputations for being light on their feet, his paws would pound on the floor. His dash would take him through every darkened room and corridor.

Then—because he couldn't keep going in a straight line—he'd sometimes slam into the walls. Usually, when he came to the wall, however, he'd skitter into a U-turn and repeat his wild dash in the other direction. Then he'd slide to a halt, lie down exhausted, and sleep through the rest of the night.

Often cats will get a sudden urge to expend their energy, have a "crazy fit," and charge madly around the house. But the run doesn't last. The cheetah, another member of the cat family and one of the fastest land animals alive, has been clocked at speeds ranging up to 50 mph, but the cheetah can't keep up this speed over long periods of time. Similarly, your cat will explode with a sudden rush and then subside, after a minute or so. A little like primal scream therapy, this is basically a release. Internal frustration, nervousness, and lack of exercise can lead a cat to erupt into sudden activity. Without a dash around the house, he might channel his energy into excessive licking, clawing, or other destructive habits. Therefore, whenever your cat looks nervous, tense, or "wired," encourage him to run around.

Hours of darkness are not the ideal time to encourage this particular pastime. While the middle of the night *is* frequently the time when cats get active, it is also the time

Hours of darkness are not ideal for this particular pastime

when most owners are sleeping. The ideal time for this game is when both man and beast are wide awake. Rather than letting him run wild by himself, initiating the run and working it through with him is your best bet. This is one of the best exercises your cat can enjoy, but be sure *you* say when it should be.

Rarely will cats knock into furniture or knock over your possessions. If you're worried, however, make sure he chases through an area where he can't get into trouble. A good deep plush carpet on the floors makes a good "track."

To get your cat going, throw something for him to chase. Drag something quickly in front of him, or give him a whiff of catnip. Pretend to chase your cat yourself; anything to raise his nervous energy and get him to expend pent-up excitement.

High Jumps

How high can your cat jump? For his size, he can leap quite a distance, his back bowed and his hindlegs straight out beneath him. He can finish his leap on even the narrowest of surfaces—for example, atop a door no more than an inch wide—without losing his balance. Cats naturally enjoy high places, and yours will usually take to being held up high over your head, where he can smell and paw at the ceiling. He'll also enjoy being carried around on your shoulders (which leaves your hands free for other chores). But you'll want to clip his claws regularly, or else wear a heavy sweater or jacket—your cat uses his claws when hanging on, and whether they hurt depends on what you're wearing for him to hang on to.

Daniel, a gray domestic, has learned to use his owner's back as a trampoline to get where he wants. When she's washing the dishes, she'll see Daniel eyeing her, measuring the distance. Then he makes a quick bound off her shoulders and to the top of the breadbox atop the refrigerator. He'll also wait for her to brush her teeth, then bound to her shoulders and on to the top of the folding bathroom door. Such stunts are great exercise, but should be encouraged only if the "landing strip" is safe and not (as is a folding door) apt to close up under a suddenly-arriving feline.

The Broadloom Wall

Samantha, a wiry Burmese, got so addicted to climbing the drapes that her owner had one wall carpeted. Now she runs up to the wall, digs in with her claws, and climbs right up, like a feline fly. Visitors are always amazed and amused.

If you do decide on carpeting a wall for your cat, however, be sure he really enjoys climbing and physical activity. It is an expensive proposition, after all, and some cats really enjoy wall climbing only when you're holding them.

The Human Jungle Gym

Cats like to jump. They clearly take some pleasure out of being able to land with such precision, and many a cat will enjoy leaping back and forth over barriers like large stuffed toys, bolster pillows, and even—perhaps—your back.

If you are down on the floor exercising, as Murphy's owner was, you may get your cat to exercise along with you. When his owner is on the living room floor doing her backbends, Murphy likes to jump atop her stomach, leap down, and run beneath the arch of her back, keeping up his routine for as long as she maintains her backbend position.

Before long, Murphy was using her body as a jump rope, running under her waist when she was at the top of a push-up, and jumping over her when she was flat on the floor.

If you practice yoga or stretching exercises at home, encourage your cat to join you and "work out" his own movements. Since you and your cat are of such unequal size, however, you should lie on the floor. Dangle a piece of string. He'll start to play with it. Then drag it around your body, under your legs, through the crook of your arm.

Plain string is fine, but more interesting and exciting for your cat is to tie a toy mouse or toy bird to the end. Don't move at the same pace, but erratically—now fast, now slow, making it bounce or flutter.

Cats naturally enjoy high places

You can also hold your cat against your chest and roll over sideways, protecting him with your elbows as you roll over him. He may put up a slight struggle at first, and if so, *always release your cat as soon as he wants to get free!* Trying to restrain him in the assurance that he'll "grow to like it" will only ensure you a fearful, reticent cat who's afraid to play with you.

Sofa Toss (The Flying Tiger)

Many people think that a cat wants only gentle treatment. Wrong! A cat is an extremely physical animal who loves a little rough-and-tumble. This doesn't mean violence, just a little rough handling.

If he were out in the wild, he would be jumping from place to place, stalking through high grass and shrubbery, tussling with some other cats, and capturing wild creatures for food. He is built for this kind of physical activity and handling; without it, he'll go soft, and become sedentary and bored.

When dropped from even a very short distance, cats always land on their feet. If you want to try this as an experiment or as a game, drop him on a cushion, bed, or very soft couch to be sure he's safe.

The feeling of sinking into something soft that gives on contact is just what the doctor ordered. Pick up your cat and throw him into a nest of soft pillows, or the corner of a deeply-stuffed couch. He'll usually come jumping back for you to throw him again. He doesn't want to get hurt, but does enjoy being thrown around.

Don't go overboard; let *him* indicate to you how much is enough. If he doesn't like it, he won't come back for more. You can't insist or demand. And if your cat doesn't feel he's in control, he's not going to enjoy himself.

6. GAMES OF
HIDE-AND-SEEK

There's no need to set up formal games of hide-and-seek, since cats will play them without your coaxing.

It's great fun for your cat to think he has you fooled about where he is. He'll hide; and when you call his name, he'll pretend he doesn't hear. It might seem silly for him to think he can fool you on your own turf. But don't be deceived; he is aware of the "gameness" of the game. He'll wait intently while you search for him. If you should tire of the game before he does, he won't let you quit. Instead, when he fears you're losing interest, he'll quickly run by you, show a glimpse of his tail, or meow to make you start looking for him again. (If you *can't* find your cat, look on the upper shelf of your closet. Cats love to climb. If you live in an apartment building and he's not in the house, look for him on the highest floor.)

Making-the-Bed Game

Once your cat sees you throwing the first sheet over the bed, he will dodge underneath it. When he does, ask "Where's Kitty?" *And keep on making the bed.*

Your cat won't move. In fact, you'll find that you can tuck the entire sheet under the mattress—even the fitted kind—and your cat will still remain in the same position.

Continue to ignore him. Soon he'll start moving his head around. When he does, call out his name. "Where's that cat? I saw him here a minute ago..." Soon his head will duck down and tilt. You can tell he's listening. "I wonder where the cat can be! He was on the bed the last time I saw him."

Soon he'll be ducking his head around, searching for the exit. "I'm sure the cat's under here somewhere..." Feel around the bed, pretending you can't see the lump of his body under the sheets. He'll start wriggling around, either trying to hide from your searching hands or to find a way out.

Keep up this pretense for as long as you want. When both you and he are bored or have had enough, lift up a corner of the sheets and blankets.

When you see him, act surprised. "Why, *there* you are, you little rascal! You really had me fooled."

Once you let him out from under the sheet, he'll probably run off. But when you are putting on the top blanket or bedspread, he'll probably be back for a reprise.

Letting the Cat Into the Bag

Buying groceries from the supermarket or going shopping at the department store means bringing home bags or boxes.

For your cat, *anything* new in his territory creates interest. The old saying, "Curiosity killed the cat; satisfaction brought him back," is absolutely valid. Your cat has to not just investigate everything, but possess and control. A bag or box forms a special little cave that is all his, and the smell of groceries and vegetables will stimulate tremendous curiosity. He will run into a bag; if there's a box open on the floor, he'll jump in.

When he's in there, ignore him. (If you don't want to play with your cat at the moment, just being in the bag or box will be satisfaction enough for him.)

Then after a few minutes, start to look for him, being sure to announce your intentions out loud. "Where *is* the cat? I saw him a few minutes ago. Where could he be?" He'll keep perfectly still at this point. He can tell when you're kidding and enjoys a joke. Perhaps he feels that he's deceiving you. Or does he *know* that you're fooling him and is going along and humoring you anyway?

Keep pretending to search for your cat. Finally pick up the box or bag, as if to throw it out. "*My*, this feels heavy!" Look inside and make eye contact with your cat. Act surprised. "What you *you* doing here?" He will jump out or wait for a pat.

The Newspaper Tent

The newspaper is something new for your cat—and as such, needs to be investigated. You are flipping the pages over, and *nothing* is more annoying to a cat than to have you ignore him when he wants attention. He'll try sitting on the page you're reading, or hiding under the newspaper sections as you spread them out.

Pippin, a seal-point Siamese, was hiding beneath the Sunday Times, sitting perfectly still. One giveaway, though: Pippin's tail protruded from under the paper. When the cat realized he'd blown his "cover," he gingerly reached out his paw and pulled his own tail back under the paper.

You'll *know* where your cat is, just as you did when he was under the bedsheets. But keep up your pretense. "Where's the cat?" But half the fun of hiding is getting found again! So gently "tag" the occasional tail or paw that protrudes from under the paper. You'll usually hear a startled meow and get "tagged" back—or have your hand dragged under the newsprint and given an affectionate bite.

Eventually find the rest of him. "*There* you are. You really had *me* fooled!" Then start turning the pages letting him hide again.

To end the game, just pick up the papers or put them in a neat pile. It can be as short a game as you want, or continue on and off for the time it takes to read the Sunday paper—often an entire week.

7. WATER SPORTS

Bubble Chasing

Bubbles will hold a cat's attention for hours just because they can't be caught. Their intangibleness is really baffling. And the way bubbles are constantly moving, changing shape, and adjusting color attracts any cat's attention.

Get yourself a jar of that bubble solution sold in the five-and-dime and in children's toy stores. (The best type of bubble solution to get is imported from Germany. The domestic kind is usually not the best, but you can make your own if you use a good soap base. For giant bubbles, add a few drops of glycerin.) Dip in the plastic circle holder that comes with the jar, making sure not to pick up so much liquid that it drips all over the place. To make bubbles, either blow through the holder or waft it in the air. Your cat will be fascinated by the bubbles, and it won't be long before he is batting away at them with his paws. When they burst on contact and disappear, he'll look at his paw in disbelief.

Don't always blow in the same direction. Keep your cat moving. He won't be able to believe he never gets anything with those quick swipes, and his determination will keep him going. *Record time*: five hours; ten containers of bubble solution: four different people taking turns. Oatmeal, the cat, never got tired; the people did and no bubble solution was left.

Angelina is a fat white Angora with big blue eyes. She's fluffy and soft and relishes luxury. Her favorite "activity" is lounging on her lace pillow in her special bed (really a baby's crib converted to a mini-bed for her), or on the back of the couch, observing everything around her. A real princess of a cat, she isn't much into physical activity and game playing.

But her owner takes bubble baths to relax at night—and Angelina jumps up to catch the foam that wafts up from the bathtub. Her owner fills the tub up to the brim to make sure there is a large accumulation of bubbles. Then she gently blows them away from the tub toward Angelina, who swats out as the foam floats above her head.

When you take a bubble bath, turn the tap on strong for a really good lather.

Leave the door to the bathroom slightly ajar and get into the tub. Make some enticing noises or call, "What's that?" You cat's innate curiosity will bring him in to see what's going on, and he won't be able to resist. Keep scratching on the wall, whistling, or making cooing sounds until your cat comes in to see what is going on.

Once he is in the bathroom, blow some froth toward him. Pick up some bubbles with your hands and toss them up in the air.

Every cat will have a different approach to these bubbles. Yours may be content to sit on the edge of the tub or on the sink, watching the panorama or hitting out at a floating bubble. Other cats will go wild and start jumping on their hind legs to catch the foam. This is different from bubble blowing; bubble-bath foam is longer lasting, and its sheer quantity is enough to fascinate your cat.

The Shower Curtain Safari

Cats may not like getting wet, but they are fascinated by that motion of the shower curtain as the water belts against it.

No cat can overcome his curiosity about what's going on behind there! He'll think you're having great fun and want to join you. He won't want to come into the shower with you, but he will enjoy the idea of being incognito on the other side of the curtain. Not only will he be mysteriously hidden, but he won't get wet.

Cats usually wander around the rim of the tub,

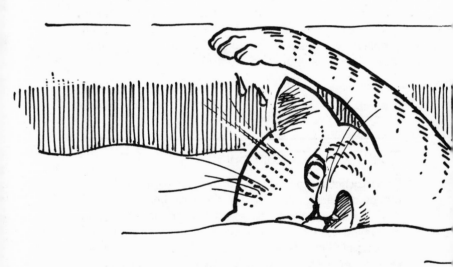

Buy him an Olympic-size swimming pool

What's going on behind the shower curtain?

scratching on the curtain. In response, you can squirt a steady steam of water from the shower against the curtain or bat it gently with your hand. But if he lunges with his claws open, he may tear the shower curtain. So move the spray of water around; move your hand from place to place to keep *him* moving.

If you have a double shower curtain—one with an opaque liner, behind which you are really shadowy—your cat might love to prowl between these two barriers. It makes it so much more exciting to explore a "tunnel." If he jumps in between the curtains or runs along the edge of the tub, don't worry—he's got excellent balance and he can stand on his hind legs on the edge of the tub and not fall in.

The Hypnotic Trickle

Alice, a white shorthair, never drinks out of a bowl. She will partake only of fresh running water—ever since the morning when her owner forgot to turn off the faucet completely and left a trickle of water running into the kitchen sink. Alice waits around in the kitchen for her owner to turn on the water. Then she jumps up onto the side of the sink, stretches her head over, and laps at the running water. She plays "footsy," pawing at the trickling stream, making a vain attempt at capturing the elusive water. Sometimes she'll lick the moisture off her paw. Then she'll go back to hitting at the water and splashing small drops around. Her owner had thought of putting straight handles on the faucets so Alice could turn them on at will, but she decided against it—Alice might flood the kitchen and besides, a small, smooth trickle is the only amount of water that's any fun.

The cost of water is on the rise, so playing with the faucet should be a special treat, in the morning when you're shaving or in the evening when you're cooking—and, of course, should be avoided in times of drought. Turn the water on ever so lightly. Your cat's fear of water is not enough to keep him from this game. Besides, not all cats hate water! Jaguars play in it and are great salmon hunters, grabbing the fish with their claws straight out of the rushing stream. He'll tentatively stick his paw out to see what the water is. If he doesn't the first time, his interest will eventually bring him around. You may not even have to entice him. Then turn away and ignore the water and him—leaving the water running, of course.

Soon he'll be trying to grab at the stream, flipping water all over, drinking, or just sitting and watching, with his head cocked to one side, as if hypnotized. If you give him the opportunity, he'll play at this for hours on end.

8. HUNTING GAMES

In the wild, cats have to hunt for survival. Even though your cat doesn't *have* to bother catching food around the house, all those millions of years of instinct ensure that he will react to anything that moves. After all, if something's not kicking, it's usually not alive—and usually not edible. This means an object doesn't have to look like possible catfood, it just has to be in motion to trigger hunting behavior.

Toe Tag

One of our clients telephoned us to complain that in the middle of the night, her cat kept pouncing on her feet and waking her up. After a little investigation, we found that the woman's toes twitched after she fell asleep. As you know, cats can see in the dark and, unless taught to sleep through the night, are active after sundown. So when her cat saw the wiggling under the blankets, he pounced.

This nightly "game" was only reinforced because she had been sticking her hand under the blanket and wiggling it around, teasing her cat to come and play. Of course, she never realized that her cat would generalize this pastime from fingers to toes, from day to night. Her solution was to buy one of those special blanket frames that lifts the bedclothes up off an injured foot.

Cats are creatures of habit. If a cat constantly finds a particular place to be a good hunting spot, you'd better believe that he'll be back again in that same spot at approximately the same time each day, looking for the same reward. This means that if you play a game of string chase with your cat in your living room at 7:30 P.M. one evening, he'll be in the living room at 7:30 the next night, ready for a rematch. So before playing "bedroom games," make sure your pet will not want to keep playing after lights out.

The best times to play toe tag are in the evening *before* going to bed, in the morning after you get up, or when lounging around on Saturday or Sunday mornings. Just start twiddling the toes of one foot under the blankets. At first your cat will watch in fascination, then he'll start to investigate by gently pawing.

Then tease him. Give a little wiggle and stop playing for a moment. He'll sit and watch, waiting for you to move again. When you think he's beginning to lose interest, twiddle your toes again. Soon he'll be pouncing on you as soon as you move. Then switch the action from one foot to the other. Your cat will cock his head from side to side and watch, waiting for the moment he thinks is right, then leap. You can bring hands into the game too, but don't get him so carried away that he starts biting. You want a gentle tussle, not an all-out teeth-and-claw war.

Blind Cat's Bluff

One study revealed that free-roaming cats tend to hang out where their prey is likely to be found. If their keen eyes detect any motion, they will sit around for hours on end, awaiting further developments. But neither you nor your cat are likely to need that kind of patience if you *make* things happen.

Leave the door ajar between two rooms, and stick your fingers through the remaining crack. Drum a couple of fingers against the jamb to attract your cat's attention. When he comes to investigate, pull your hand slowly back through the door, keeping your fingers wiggling.

He'll soon stick his paw around the door to try to snag your fingers—usually while keeping himself hidden behind the door. (Where do you think the term copy*cat* came from?) When you tag his paw, he'll probably pull it back—

Sublet to mice

but after a few moments, will soon push it out again trying to tag you or waiting for your response.

Cats like this game because *they* initiate it. There are endless variations, wherever your cat can place himself so that his paw is visible but the rest of him isn't—under a bed with a spread that sweeps the floor, inside a paper bag, or under a newspaper tent. Most cats prefer to go "blind," feeling with their paws for the fingers they could easily glimpse if only they poked their heads out. But this way, it's more fun.

This game does need a couple of definite rules. Your cat should not be "allowed" to peek or to use more than his forepaw. You, on the other hand, should be quick enough to avoid his making frequent contact and getting bored.

Even more enticing is when he doesn't always feel it's your finger tagging him back. Use long feathers, cotton swabs, shoehorns—anything with a different texture than your hand. The constantly changing sensations will leave your cat positively fascinated. The game ends when he's finally tempted to peek and see what's going on.

Blarney, a flame-tipped Himalayan, is infatuated with this game, convinced there's a "door prize" behind his owner's dressing room door. The dressing room has been off limits to Blarney ever since he sharpened his claws on a new leather jacket, so he really doesn't know what may be inside there. Finally, when his desire to play the game intensified, he used to sit outside the door, meowing and scratching, and his owner had to continue the game on more familiar turf. Changing the location of play from one room to another usually won't upset a cat. He'll investigate most doors on a regular basis and think that only on occasion is "prey" hanging out behind any one.

A more comfortable variation is to use a large, overstuffed chair. Place your cat in the seat, then sit or stand behind the chair. Sneak your fingers around one side. When you're tagged, retreat and approach from the other side of the chair. Your cat will enjoy trying to guess where you're coming from next.

Cushion Retrieval

Blind Cat's Bluff is closely related to a cat's hunting instincts: Wild cats place their paws down a mousehole and feel around, trying to snag the rodent inside, and chase it out. Therefore, your cat will adore imitation mouseholes—especially the cleft between old sofa cushions. Place a small plastic knotball in there, and your cat will run to pull it out, often throwing it up in the air before clasping it in his teeth or between his paws.

This game is somewhat boring from *your* point of view, because there's little challenge to shoving a bit of damp plastic into your sofa. But your cat will be happy to keep it up as long as you do.

Stalking the Wild Feather Duster

One secretary finds she can give her cat, Whiskers, some good exercise with one of those feather dusters that are so convenient for getting into hard-to-reach places. She waves this duster in front of Whiskers, and he jumps for it. When she tickles him with it, Whiskers rolls over, scratching at the feathers with his paw. Even if not actually offered the duster, he will try to grab for it—sometimes leaping high up in the air.

It's probably the duster's fluttery motion and soft texture that make it enticing. So, to keep your cat interested, you've got to keep the duster active. Whiskers' owner reports that her cat keeps following her around while she's dusting and is reluctant to see her put the feather duster away.

Tug of Paw

When playing with your cat, take a long piece of cloth, a dish towel or a belt (leather belts are a bit heavy, but the belt of an old terry cloth bathrobe is ideal) and tie a big knot in one end. Flip it out toward your pet and wriggle it back and forth like a whip. Cats use their front paws for handling and grasping as well as for walking. And most every cat loves to use his retractable claws to dig into things and grab hold. Even a declawed cat will still use his paws as if they had "blades." When he goes to grab at it with his paws, flip it farther, and then draw it quickly back. Let it slip through his paws. Then suddenly pause, and watch him wait for you to move it again. When you do, he'll embrace it, and probably even bite at it with his teeth. Tug on one end and let him tug on the other. Pretend to really struggle. Make grunting noises to let him think he's really strong.

Set up a barrier over which either he or you must pass. A doorway is a fine demarcation line, as is the edge of a rug or on/off a chair.

But "winning" in this case means gaining control of the tugged object—the cloth. Your cat will adore this little test of physical power. This does not mean that it is a game of absolute control. Neither of you should win *all* the time, or there will be discontent on both sides.

The Tail Decoy

In the wild, standard body language movements and reactions accompany the intrusion of one cat into another's territory. Often there are pathways through which passage is allowed. This is why most cats will go on guard, waiting for an intruder to crouch in submission or slowly walk past and away. If the intruder keeps up a boastful "tails up" attitude, however, the cat whose territory is being invaded will move to protect it.

How does your cat feel about other cats? Does he like them, dislike them, act ambivalent, or just curious? Each cat may have a different way of responding in this game. But that doesn't matter. *Any* reaction is fine, as long as there is one.

Get a strip of fur or dark velvet that looks like a cat's tail and attach it to a dowel or pencil so that it sticks stiffly up in the air. Secrete yourself behind a couch or other such barrier where you can observe your cat's reactions. Hold the tail up so that it projects above the edge of the barrier. To attract your cat's attention, mimic the cry of a plaintive, angry, or defiant feline.

Some cats will hunch up, hair bristling, and tensely approach, hissing and striking out at the tail. A female in heat, a horny male, or a friendly, submissive cat may come over solicitously, purring and rubbing against the furniture. But slow wariness is the most usual reaction.

Most often your cat will circle around, tail in the air, to see what kind of reaction *he'll* get. Some cats may even run and hide in indignation. If you wiggle the tail around and make the right noises, however, you should get a reaction. Once he finds out it's you on the other end of the tail, his knowledge that it *is* you will make the game even more fun.

Caution: Don't play this game with any cat that really hates other felines. The owner of Honeysuckle didn't know how violent his cat's reaction would be. On seeing the other "cat's" tail, Honeysuckle quickly ran behind the couch and grabbed hold of her owner's leg, clawing and biting.

Shadows in the Night

This is a perfect evening game. Get hold of a strong flashlight or a slide projector, turn off the lights. Flash the light on a blank wall and prop up the light source so that your hands are free. Now play shadow games as you did when you were a child, making rabbits, chickens, snakes, and any other creatures you can. Any object you hang in front of the light will cast its magnified shadow on the wall, but *huge* shadows may make your cat want to run away. Play with him by making them approach and retreat. You'll be able to do this simply enough and if he's right next to the wall the smaller, "bite size" shadows will attract your cat's attention. Soon he'll be leaping up at the wall, trying to catch hold of the elusive shapes.

Hand-created shadows are best since they give you the freedom to interact with your cat. But felines may enjoy this game more than human offspring. One woman was entertaining both her children and their cats. She made a bat shadow by hooking her thumbs together and flapping her fingers to simulate wings in flight. She made a snake by holding her fingers close together, tucking in the thumb, and twisting her arm.

The cats were fascinated. But that night—and for several nights thereafter—her youngest son woke up screaming with nightmares about bats and snakes. This mother no longer plays shadow games with her children. She saves them for the cats, when the kids are tucked in and fast asleep.

Let your cat cast his own shadow

9. MORE ADVANCED BALL GAMES

CATminton

You may never be Chris Evert Lloyd or Bjorn Borg; you might not even be able to serve and volley on a tennis court at all, but you can have a great match with your cat. Your cat uses his paws for everything and has no problem returning or blocking anything you toss at him.

Start off by just scooting a ball across the floor toward your cat. Prepare a number of the homemade ones described in Chapter 3, because you don't want to have to go chasing after them—and it's for sure that there are going to be some misses.

Unless he's fast asleep, he'll run over to check it out. If he's in the least bit playful, he'll bat it with his paw, or at least "shortstop" it from rolling farther. Keep up the game and try to get him to actually return it with a slap of the paw. But don't let his refusal to return it stop your "serves." Take his position as goalie as an accomplishment in itself, and be resigned to the fact that you will need lots of balls to toss because he's not returning them.

Once you've got the game going on ground level, then get your cat to leap *up* for the balls. Just throw them slightly up in the air—at first, at a level where he stretches a little for them. Then a little higher. Lob them into a sofa or atop a bed where he has to jump to catch them.

Once your cat is really proficient, begin throwing the ball at different heights and in different directions, giving him a surprise each time.

Stand up when you throw. Now and then, kick it to him. He shouldn't just lie there, but should get moving around.

Recommendations: This game is really best for slim, short-haired cats who tend to be much more active than long-haired ones. If, of course, you have a fat, lazy Persian,

Slim, short-haired cats tend to be much more active

play it his way. Treat him like those nineteenth-century women tennis players who stood in one spot while their "gentlemen" friends hit the ball directly at them, apologizing if it went out of line just one inch.

Pawball

This is a good late-night bedtime game. A cat tends to wake up at night, so a little pre-bed exercise will help tire him out enough to help him doze—and let you sleep. It can be used along with Toe Tag as a nightcap for your cat.

In this case, an aluminum foil ball may not have enough bounce. Take a piece of clear plastic sheeting (such as a bag from the cleaners or the wrapper that covers the Sunday newspaper) and knot it up several times. Then snip off the ends. The resulting ball-like shape is soft enough for your cat to play with, and won't hurt your walls or furnishings. Toss it up over the bed and let it bounce off the wall. Your cat will jump up, trying to catch it in midair. He will either bat it with one paw or grasp it between both paws and carry it to his mouth. Some cats will bat it back and forth on the bed for a few minutes. Then they will let you have it back when they want you to start the game over.

Of course, your cat will like this straightforward game even better if you get a little animated and show proper enthusiasm. Don't let your cat catch the ball every time. Sometimes grab it yourself before he can reach it. Pretend to hide the ball from him, and then bring it out from nowhere. Feinting—pretending to toss it a couple of times before actually doing so—will get him more excited. Ask, "Are you ready?" Cats enjoy some anticipation. And a simple straightforward throwing of the "ball" against the wall for him to catch can be a bore.

Use "corner shots" that bounce off the ceiling, "drop

An aluminum foil ball may not have enough bounce

shots" that hit high on the wall and fall nearly straight down. Go to the foot of the bed and throw a low line drive over your cat's head—a shot that's easy for him to intercept. If he in turn begins playing the Gravity Game—throwing the ball off the bed and onto the floor—you should stop play immediately. You don't want him to start clearing off the tops of shelves and tables! The ball is "in play" only as long as it remains on the bed.

Fetching and Retrieving

Hunting is not something that comes as second nature to a cat. If a kitten stays with his mother, she will teach him to hunt, but the young cat does not learn this lesson until he is about nine to ten weeks old. At that point, the cat will grab an object, pretend to kill it, and return with it to help "feed" the head of the household. Unfortunately, if your cat wasn't taught by his mother through observation and then direct supervised practice, he may jump after things, but not "kill" and return them, which is the basis of this game. Some cats who never learned to hunt may retrieve; others may not.

The ancient Egyptians and more recently, the East Indians taught cheetahs and caracals to retrieve prey that had been brought down by bowmen. In some cases, the cats were even taught to catch and kill on their own, *then* retrieve. It should be noted, however, that after successful retrieving, the cat was always given some kind of reward— usually fresh blood, since that was the only thing these animals found as enticing as the prey. (In your house, a tidbit of fish might be a good reward to induce your cat to retrieve, but always keep it a game.) To play, merely toss the ball out on the floor. Once he runs after it, that's half of the fetch/retrieve game. If this is *all* he ever does, that's okay too. This is just a game for your pleasure and his, and not a rigid training session. But if he will bring it back, that saves you the bother of running after the ball each time you throw it. This is also an entirely different game. He brings the ball back for *you* to throw, rather than running off to play with it by himself.

Remember that a cat doesn't get the same pleasure from holding objects in his mouth that a dog does. Nor do most cats crave human approval as much as dogs do except, perhaps, for the more social and "doglike" Siamese. So your cat needs an additional incentive to bring back any object you throw.

Wait until he takes it in his mouth. Then you can often get him to return it by calling him, or by enticing him with a sound or action. Scratch on the floor. Make clicking sounds. Do something that interests him enough to bring it back before he drops it. Then when he comes, take the ball from his mouth and throw it out again.

Another way to get him into the habit is to prepare several balls. Throw one out. When he goes for it and takes it, throw out another. This way he'll get into the habit of

running after consecutive objects. After a while, wait between throws. You might get him to come back with the ball.

Make sure who's training whom, however. Blitz, a male
calico, will usually fetch the ball back to his owner—so long
as she's not paying him any attention. But if she looks at
Blitz, he'll drop the ball. Sure, he wants her to throw it again.
But he's learned that she'll usually go get it herself. Why
should *he* bother to lug the ball all the way back?

10. CATNIP: THE ENERGIZING ODOR

Standard Feline Reactions

That rumor about cats getting their jollies from catnip is absolutely true. Whenever his owner gives Bruce a whiff of catnip, the cat first performs a series of rolling movements on the floor and starts rubbing his chin and flanks against any objects in reach. Then he starts shaking his head, scratches wildly at the floor, and rushes madly across the room. He stops suddenly, looks around, and heads in the other direction. For a number of minutes he runs all over the house, then flops down, exhausted, only to jump up again a few minutes later and start running all over again.

Angie, a little Siamese, is also stimulated by catnip. After she's had a whiff, she stands in one spot and starts jumping straight up and down. As she leaps into the air, her claws unsheath themselves and she pounces right straight down again.

Jerry, the tabby from around the corner, gets sexually aroused by catnip and looks for any soft object he can find. First he rubs against it and then tries—in vain—to mount it. If anyone comes near and tries to interfere, he gets very upset and takes on a fighting stance. His hair stands on end and he waves his tail high in the air. Then if you approach his "love" object, he moves back and forth sideways, trying to scare you off with his fierce cries and hisses. Yet if you actually do approach, he does nothing—it all seems to be show. But once left alone, Jerry proceeds with his unrequited lovemaking.

Catnip is a member of the mint family and grows wild over a large area of America and Europe. For years domestic cat owners have purchased dried catnip leaves for use as an "exerciser" to get young kittens going or as a rejuvenator to bring old cats to new life.

Its effects are fascinating to watch. Wild animal hunt-

*That rumor about cats getting their jollies from catnip
is absolutely true*

ers and photographers use it to get members of the cat
family into position where they can be caught—physically
or on film. Animal behaviorists have studied catnip to see if
it links with sexual or hunting behavior; in fact, the profes-
sionals did a big study on the subject, which was summed
up in a paper, "Catnip and Oestrous Behavior in the Cat"
printed in *Animal Behavior* magazine (V14, 1966). This
study was based on several other studies that had been
done many years earlier, and further work has been done
even more recently. But to this day, these experiments have
yielded no conclusive results. It *is* definitely known that not
every cat will respond to catnip, and that catnip's odor, and
not its taste, causes the reaction.

When catnip is offered, most cats sniff at it, and then
start rubbing their faces into the leaves and rolling back and
forth over them. Some cats will eat it as well, scratch
around, dig, and beg for more. Catnip gets a cat more active
than ever, more prone to get involved in physical feats of

This paralyzed reaction doesn't seem to be unusual

one sort or another. But any individual cat's exact reaction to this substance is not definitely predictable. It depends on your cat's temperament, what kind of mood he's in at the time, or what's on his mind and what interests him. Usually he will be physically more attuned than normal and a little hyperactive. He will display intensified or otherwise unexpected reactions because his inhibitions have been loosened and the intoxication acts as a stimulant.

Catnip is great to administer to your cat just before getting into a really good rough-and-tumble game. Generally he will perk up, sharpen his senses, and get in the mood for whatever game *you* want to play. It is available commercially in most pet shops and in herb or health-food stores. You can get a toy or ball with the dried-up leaves hidden inside, so the catnip odor will keep your cat playing for hours.

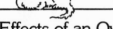

Effects of an Overdose

Smitty, a black longhair, got into a jar of catnip leaves. For three hours he lay perfectly still, staring at the picture of a parrot which his owner had in her kitchen—apparently waiting for the bird to move so that he could pounce.

This paralyzed, staring reaction doesn't seem to be an unusual reaction in cases of catnip overdose. Several people have reported such behavior: One female cat stood and stared at TV for two hours without moving. Another smoky male sat on the top shelf of a bookcase, staring at a plant across the room for forty-five minutes. Still another little male sat and stared out of the window for an hour and a half. This *cata*tonic state doesn't appear to be harmful, but can be quite unnerving to an uninformed owner. As you know, "straight" cats will sometimes sit and stare for a few minutes at a time, but the catnip seems to intensify and extend the reaction. Ordinarily, a staring cat will wiggle one ear, turn his head, or display some kind of movement. With a catnip overdose, however, complete stillness is sometimes observed.

Catnip is generally considered to be a stimulant, which is why this paralytic reaction seems so out of line with the normal effects. Since catnip does affect the feline nervous system, it may simply intensify what would be a normal stalking reaction. The overdosed cat gets so mentally wrapped up that for him, time stands still. Because the long-range effects of catnip are unknown, you shouldn't engage your cat in regular daily doses of the stuff. Treat him as you should yourself, and let him get his relaxation in moderate doses.

11. RIDES

The Weightless Wheelbarrow

When you were a kid, remember such competitions as the Three-legged Race, the Sack Race, and The Egg-and-Spoon Race? The Wheelbarrow was equally ungraceful, but a lot of laughs. One person grabbed another's ankles and lifted them until the other was practically horizontal and had to support himself on his hands. The ankle holder then walked forward slowly, while the "wheelbarrow" was forced to stumble along on his hands, as fast as he could.

Your cat is *already* horizontal, however, so the wheelbarrow stunt won't much appeal to him. In fact, holding his hindquarters off the floor will make a long-spined cat uncomfortable. So you have to adapt the Wheelbarrow into an activity he likes to perform.

One thing your cat cannot do is climb the wall, or walk across the ceiling. But he can if you cradle the lower part of your cat's back and hold him sideways so his front paws rest against the wall. When he goes to "walk" forward, let him—as if his hindquarters were being dragged along automatically.

There's nothing a cat likes more than for you to get on the ground and be his equal, or to let him rise to yours. Being wheeled on walls makes him feel as if he were involved in some real daredevil physical activity, and he can sniff and investigate picture frames, thermostats, and all sorts of things inaccessible from the ground. Hold him securely under his hips and shoulders, and he can even walk on the ceiling! But always press him closely enough so he can walk without slipping.

Hold him securely under his hips and shoulders

Snap the Cat

If you've ever watched kittens playing with each other, you've noticed that one of their favorite games is to tug each other around, especially on an incline or slippery surface. You can give your adult cat the same amusement. One woman built a wooden ramp down from the top of her cat's scratching post. The wood is highly polished, and Satin seems to enjoy sliding down it. But that's a Solitaire game; it's much more enjoyable to interact with your feline.

If the room has linoleum or a bare hardwood floor, seat your cat on a scrap of carpet or an old (but clean) dish towel and tug him around. You can also teach him to dig in his claws—as in a game of Tug of Paw—and let himself be dragged across the floor.

If he likes roughhousing, you can even play Snap the Cat, letting him slide some distance on his own. Try to arrange things so that he lands in a soft cushion, preferably stuffed with down. But if your room is carpeted, a low cardboard box may be the answer. That is, a "cart" that slides easily over the carpeting. It won't be too comfortable for you to crawl about the rug, though, so a rope or tether is perfectly acceptable. This way you can stand up and still pull your cat about the house. Soon your cat will go over to his towel or box and meow, waiting for you to supply the propulsion. But to overcome the inertia of a several-pound cat, you may need a quick, decisive yank to get him moving. But don't pull so quickly—or so hard—that your cat is jerked off his feet. At first, it's better to just pull, slowly and steadily, until the "toboggan" begins to move.

Loop the Kitten (The Centrifugal Cat)

Remember in General Science, when the teacher dazzled you by swirling an open pail of water round on the end of a string—without losing one drop? Remember the Roto-Reel in the amusement park? You and other paying customers stood inside a big drum, which began to revolve, the centrifugal force flattening you against the wall. Then the floor beneath you descended, but you remained flattened against the wall, apparently defying gravity.

Loop the Kitten is one of those amusements your cat will beg you to play with him. For this stunt, you need a pair of *strong* paper shopping bags, one fitted inside the other, or else a single cloth or leather bag with strong handles. Put him into the bag, or just leave it standing around—curiosity will make him jump in all by himself. When he's inside, pick up the bag by *both* handles and swing it from side to side like a pendulum. Build up the length of the arc, and every once in a while, swing it over your head, through a complete circle. Be sure that you do this *decisively* and fast enough to create enough centifugal force to keep him in the bag.

Once your centrifugal cat gets a taste of this game, he'll enjoy it so much that he'll jump into every bag he sees, meow to get your attention, and wait to get you to swing him around. The quick physical thrill is irresistible. The owners of Francine, a three-year-old Siamese, report that she is so addicted to the centrifugal fix that she can't go for more than a day without an overhead spin. She climbs into her favorite swing bag and wails with that loud, piercing cry so typical of a Siamese.

Caution: Some cats object to this kind of physical insecurity. (There *are* some people who don't enjoy amusement park rides.) So ease your cat into centrifugalization to be sure if it's his dish of cream. Also, you've got to be sure not to frighten or injure him. If you don't perform the flip quickly enough, your cat will go into free fall, or at least feel momentarily weightless—a most unsettling sensation.

12. CONTESTS

Broken Field Tackling

This game is a combination of open field tackling and broken field running—as you know from football.

In tackling, one offensive player tries to reach the goal line, and one defensive man tries to prevent him. In broken field running, the man carrying the ball, instead of running a straight line, zigzags down the field to avoid blockers. Combine the two, and you get Broken Field Tackling.

To play, get down on the floor and face off with your cat. Toss a ball toward him. He may or may not hit it back to you, depending on his inclination, dexterity, and eye and paw coordination. After you've got your cat pushing this ball back and forth (and even if he doesn't!) take the ball between your hands and bounce it back and forth between them. If your cat is really into the game, he should try to snatch it away with his paw.

Your job is to prevent him—and to move the ball and your body past him without him stopping you with a "tackle." (Once he tags you, drop the ball.) Weave back and forth around the furniture. Set yourself a goal line *you* have to cross in order to win—a doorway is always a good definite barrier. Even if your cat can't really get the ball away from you, let him tag you and make you drop the ball from time to time to make the game interesting.

When your cat gets the ball, encourage him to move with it down the "field" in the other direction. Pretending to block his way, tackle him gently and take the ball away from him. Play gently with him until he has really got the idea of the game down pat and is enthusiastic about retaining the ball and moving it across the floor.

This game takes a little time and practice, but most cats have the brains and physical ability to do it. Of course, keep in mind that some cats don't like getting involved in

Teach him to bowl

complicated games. They want a quick. silly contest, and that's it. This is why you should start things off simple and build them up if your cat wants. Don't push him. Always remember that a game is intended for fun, not for training, rules, and regulations. If your cat enjoys a game, fine; if not, make it more basic or go on to something else.

Batting Practice

This is a truly competitive form of Pawball in which you serve as an automatic ball-feeding machine for your cat. You *may* want to field the balls he whaps at you but if so, you'll need a bit of practice if you want to score better than .325.

Place your cat up on a shelf or atop the refrigerator—wherever he can sit comfortably, at about your eye level. Then take a knotted plastic ball and throw it *straight up* in front of your cat, within a six-inch "strike zone" of his nose.

A cat is superbly equipped to follow movement, so he'll need only a few up-and-down passes before he's able to swat the ball out of the air at the top of its arc. If you try to retrieve the ball before it hits the floor, you'll be hard pressed to catch every shot. The challenge of the swiftly-moving ball delights cats. Some will sit up, purring with pleasure, until the ball shoots by, and then knock it out of the air every time.

Warning: This physical-activity game involves agility of movement—both you and your cat have to be in good shape. But if you're not, after playing this game for a while, you soon will be. If you get lazy, it's tempting to just place the ball on the shelf and have your cat knock it off. This does make it easier for you to catch, but it also encourages your cat to play the Gravity Game.

Record: Michael and Alleykazam played this game for six hours straight. Alley finally came away the victor. He returned the balls almost consecutively. Mike ran himself ragged trying to return his cat's returns, which Alley skillfully placed just out of reach. Mike never asked for a rematch, and has been playing different cat games in the hopes of finding one he's good at.

The Shell Game

This is just what it sounds like—the standard shell game done in bars and on street corners. When you come to playing it with your cat, however, it isn't such a sucker's game. Cats have such keen sight that they have no problem following that one shell with the pea underneath it.

Your problem is that a mere pea under a shell isn't usually enough to motivate your cat into getting excited about this game. After all, *people* don't play shell games for peas. They play for cash. And not every cat will play this game. Often it takes a "gambler" type; some cats quickly develop the habit of taking a chance on the possibility of a reward. But even a nongambling feline may well do it for the fun of the challenge: to show he's faster than you. Besides, it's an intense one-on-one contest for cat and owner, a question of who can psych out whom.

Equipment: Take three identical "shells"—small bowls, opaque paper cups, plastic shaving cream can lids, empty cat food cans, or any other small, manipulatable containers. Sit your cat on the floor or table in front of you and start pushing two of the shells around. Get his attention by asking him, "What's that?" Let him see and smell the interior of the two shells. Then your cat has to be shown what he's "betting" on. You can use a food reward. Either hide a piece of dry food under one shell, or quickly give one to your cat as soon as he locates the pea. Some cats will even play if your put a favorite toy underneath the "shell."

Wiggle the object around in your fingers. Crunch it against the floor so it makes noises. Pretend it is exotic and mysterious and possibly unattainable. Switch it from hand to hand. Hide it, then bring it out. Throw it in the air and catch it. If *you* play with it, he'll want to try it himself.

Once he's really paying attention, hide it under one of the "shells." Switch them around. After you stop, pick up the shell with the object underneath it (that is, if *you* still know). Give him the treat, or let him play briefly with the toy. Do it again, but this time, wait and see if he'll go for the "shell" with the object under it, either by nosing or pawing at it.

Even if you do use a scented object under the shell, his sense won't help him find it. Even though cats sniff everything, their olfactory sense is not as developed as a dog's.

In fact, to get a good "whiff," your cat has to open his mouth and rely on his Jacobson's organ—an olfactory structure in the mouth, rather than in the nasal passage. Like the humans who play this game, cats have to rely on eyesight to follow the right shell. But since their vision is so exceptionally atuned to movement, they'll probably be able to keep close tabs on the "pea" far better than the best human player.

Once he gets the idea and is fairly successful, go to three shells. Sometimes he'll win, sometimes he'll lose. But as long as you keep up the action and make it interesting, he'll keep playing.

Record: Fat Cat, a male Burmese, wins at this game 90 percent of the time (the average correct response is at the 60 percent level).

13.
PSYCHOLOGISTS' GAMES

Animal-behavior students have invented a variety of ways to test cats' reaction time, eye coordination, muscle movements, skeletal idiosyncrasies, hearing ability, acuity of smell and taste, chase reactions, and so on. In addition to all they have taught us about a cat's physiognomy and behavioral workings, these experiments serve as the inspiration for several games that will challenge, entertain, and amuse your cat. (In case a friend questions who has the smartest cat, these games could provide the answer.)

The Maze

In psychology laboratories, this is perhaps the most widely used test for measuring intelligence, learning, and habit formation in every sort of animal—from rats to cats to mice to people. Mazes are also used to permit competition between animals of different backgrounds and characteristics. A long-haired, mixed-breed kitten with green eyes who's been with his mother for three months might be pitted against a short-haired, blue-eyed Siamese who only saw his mother a few days before he was orphaned.

The standard laboratory maze used for cats is the standard T-type. Psychologists have found they can't use *completely* enclosed mazes, however, since that produces fear in felines. The cat doesn't want to risk a one-way trip, and refuses to budge. Unlike rats and mice, who live in burrows and so do fine in blind-wall mazes, cats rely on sight. They prefer to have some visual or auditory orientation. Therefore, cat-testing mazes tend to be made of chicken wire mesh or some similar material. In your house, you can rearrange cardboard boxes or use lengths of plywood to build a temporary maze.

To motivate your cat to get going around the maze, entice him with an unusual noise at the exit. His sense of

Hidden in his lair, waiting for prey

hearing is especially keen, and his ears will swivel around to pinpoint the source of the sound. Once he thinks the noise interesting enough, he'll move in. A reward of some sort such as a tidbit at the exit makes the whole journey more worthwhile.

Another way to get your cat through the maze is to drag a toy on the end of a string in front of him. This is cheating, of course: It won't allow you to test your cat's intelligence, but it will show you how fast he can move.

The Skinner Play Box

Behavioral psychologists use this teaching aid, invented by B.F. Skinner, to teach animals to perform an action that brings a desired reward—or conversely, avoids an undesirable punishment. Usually the creatures learn simply to press down on a lever that releases a food tidbit or averts an unpleasant shock.

Once the animal has learned whatever has been expected of him, the experimenter sees how long it takes for the action to be extinguished. Slowly, the animal understands that its behavior no longer "counts" and no longer is followed by any reward. And so, the frustrated critter stops doing it.

Obviously, this routine isn't something you'd want to go through with your cat. Use the basic concept, however, and make a Skinner Play Box. All you need is a cardboard box and a cat to put in it. Instead of putting in a lever and chute for rewards, just cut a small opening three inches by four inches, at one end of the box.

Put your cat into the box, or let him crawl in on his own. Tie a toy to a string and swing it gently across the opening. The movement of something flashing across his field of vision will grab his attention. Before long your cat will stick his nose out to see what's going on. Then swing the toy closer. Soon he'll be sticking out his paw and trying to pull it back through the hole. The point of the game is to see whether your cat can grab the toy as it goes by. This means that at first, you should move it at a reasonably slow speed so that he has the opportunity to grasp it. But at the same time, don't just give it to him. Adjust the game to fit his abilities. Soon the practice will sharpen your cat's reaction time and paw manipulation.

If you can plug up the box's opening in some way, your cat will have to initiate the game by pushing it open again by himself. Hinge the opening by cutting only three sides of the hole, or by taping one side of the cut-out section back in place. Or you can put a curtain over the hole—but make it light, translucent cloth that your cat can easily push aside with his paw. Eventually, he'll crawl in the box and stick his paw through the hole to alert you that he's ready to play.

After he gets proficient at the game, you can give your

cat more control. Use a box topped with only a piece of light cardboard. While he lies hidden, bump the toy on the "lid." This way he'll pounce up like a jack-in-the-box to grab it. Don't worry, your cat won't mind being in there. He'll probably love it, feeling he is sitting hidden in his lair, waiting sneakily for prey to appear.

The Locked Cage Escape

Psychologists take advantage of the fact that cats have manipulative paws and give them various tasks that require reaching and "manual" ability. One intelligence test is to put a cat in a cage with a latched door. The experimenters open the door to let the caged cat see how the latch works, then observe to see how long it takes the cat to manipulate the latch itself, open the door, and escape. In this way, they measure:

   1. The number of times the cat needs to have an experimenter demonstrate the operation;

   2. How many times the cat needs to fiddle around with the latch before he finally opens it for the first time;

   3. How long it takes the cat to open the latch thereafter, until he masters the task and it becomes a quick one-shot procedure.

   Is there something in the house that can contain your cat, and yet give him a means of exit if he manipulates a latch of some sort? Round door knobs won't serve this function, but straight-handle types will. The push of a cat's paw should open a levered door if the spring isn't too tight. (You can also reverse the procedure: Instead of having him get *out* of a container or room, have him let himself in.) A latch has to be low enough so he can reach it readily. If you tie a string from the latch, will the correct pull from your cat get it open?

Don't make your cat so efficient that no cabinet is safe

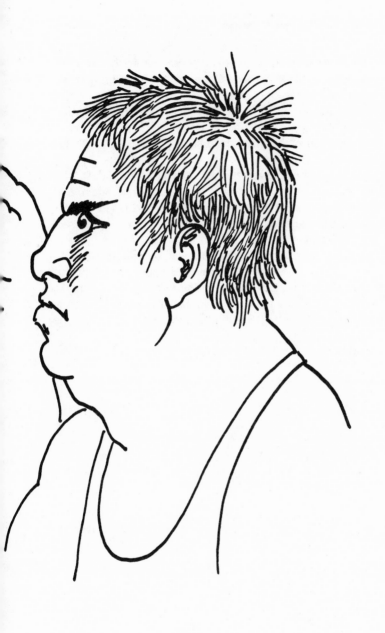

You can entice your pet into coming through any door if what's on the other side is fascinating enough. On the other side of the door, put something he really wants and make sure he sees it's there. Then demonstrate the opening procedure. Show him how to open the door; either by a simple push or by grasping a slightly open door with his paw and pulling it.

Close the door and watch to see if he tries to do it. If he doesn't attempt to open the door, demonstrate again, and again show him the goodie that's to be had when he gets through to the other side. It's really a case of monkey-see, monkey-do.

Warning: Don't make your cat so efficient that no closed closet, cabinet, or container is safe from his prying paws. Even if he *can't* open a given door, his claw marks won't do much for the paint or varnish. Never put food, toys, or any enticing objects behind a door that supposed to be verboten.

14. ELECTRICITY AND ESP

The Static-Electrified Cat

This is really a game for you and your friend(s); your cat is the instrument of the game and the recipient of the pleasure involved.

As you know, cats love a good stroking—especially around the base of the tail, the cheeks of the face, and behind the ears. (These areas contain glands that normally secrete odors. This is why they rub these areas on your legs and on furniture as they go by, to "mark" it as belonging to them.) Stroking a cat's fur also produces static electricity, which forms the basis of this game. The winner is the person who can generate the most electricity when stroking the cat. (Your cat is of course always the biggest winner, with all that stroking and attention.)

This contest is best played in the winter, when the heat is on in your house and the relative humidity is low. Attach a small Styrofoam ball to the end of a nylon thread. Rub the Styrofoam ball on the cat's back with firm strokes and then dangle it near your cat. The ball should be attracted to your cat's coat since your rubbing has added a negative charge. Opposite charges attract. Normally, the Styrofoam ball will have equal quantities of both positive and negative charges, while rubbing your cat's fur will produce an excess of negative charges. Therefore, the ball should be attracted to your cat's fur.

In the same way, you could also see if his coat can pick up a very light piece of tissue paper. A brush can also be substituted for the Styrofoam ball. Charge the ball by rubbing *it* down your cat's back. Then quickly brush your cat's fur and hold the brush next to the ball. In this case, you and your cat will see the similar electrical charges repel each other.

CATelepathy

We haven't tried this one ourselves, but we're assured it works.

Amos, a male tortoiseshell, had been an indoor cat for all of his three years—until Matt, his owner, moved to a house in the suburbs, and saw no reason why Amos should not have the run of the green, well-mowed back yard. But, Amos took such a delight in his new-found freedom that he would scratch at the door to go out at all hours of the day *and* night. Matt didn't want Amos out after dark because of the skunks, raccoons, and owls also out at that hour. But Amos, being as stubborn as cats can often be, would go back to scratching as soon as Matt rose to make him quit.

Was there a way to make Amos—in another room, out of sight—stop scratching to go out? Did Matt have to keep getting up to shoo the cat away from the front door?

In desperation, Matt turned to the occult. He reasoned that *if* cats are naturally telepathic, they probably "communicate" by strong visual images—which, after all, is the stimulus they ordinarily react to. So as precisely as possible, Matt envisioned Amos scratching at the front door. (It wasn't hard, since Amos was out in the living room, doing so at that very moment!)

Then Matt pictured himself in the scene, striding across the rug toward Amos with an angry look on his face—and envisioned Amos running away from the door.

Miraculously, out in the pitch-black living room, Amos stopped scratching.

Not believing his good fortune, Matt tried again: He envisioned his own ankles under the blankets at the bottom of the bed. Amos liked nothing better than to curl up in the soft hammock between them. Not ten seconds later, Amos

*If CATelepathy works, it promises a new closeness
between you and your cat*

jumped on the bed, headed straight for Matt's legs, and settled down between his ankles.

Now Matt uses vivid mental images to make Amos behave, and Matt claims Amos obeys far *better* to telepathy than to ordinary spoken commands. Specifically, Matt uses mind power to call Amos inside when he's about to leave the house. He vividly pictures Amos walking in the front door—and invariably, just as Matt is gathering up his overcoat and car keys, Amos shows up.

If CATelepathy really works, it promises a whole new closeness between you and your cat—and a wonderful new way of relating to animals in general. The only secret, Matt says, is to *vividly* imagine the cat doing just what you want him to—and then wipe the image from your mind. A successful "hit" will register almost immediately.